Strange ... But True?

AREA 51

KYLA STEINKRAUS

WORLD BOOK

This World Book edition of *Area 51* is published by agreement between Black Rabbit Books and World Book, Inc.
© 2018 Black Rabbit Books,
2140 Howard Dr. West,
North Mankato, MN 56003 U.S.A.
World Book, Inc.,
180 North LaSalle St., Suite 900,
Chicago, IL 60601 U.S.A.

Marysa Storm, editor; Grant Gould, interior designer; Michael Sellner, cover designer; Omay Ayres, photo researcher

Library of Congress Control Number: 2016049986

ISBN: 978-0-7166-9353-6

Printed in the United States at CG Book Printers, North Mankato, Minnesota, 56003. 3/17

Image Credits
Alamy: Bob Pardue – SC, 24–25; EuroStyle Graphics, 22 (background); Lee Dalton, 14 (blackbird); MasPix, Cover, 12–13; MC Images, 14–15 (U-2); Retro Stock Express, 21 (background); Science Picture Co, 26 (alien); Stuart Burford, 22 (text); US Air Force Photo, 15 (Nighthawk); Getty Images: DigitalGlobe/ScapeWare3d, 10–11; http://area51specialprojects.com/: TD Barnes, 9; http://rationalwiki.org/: Unknown, 18 (top); http://ufoonline.freeforumzone.com/: slickmatt03, 23; iStock: bertos, 1, Back Cover; estt, 3; fergregory, 17; Shutterstock: adike, 5 (alien); bestfoto77, 18 (bottom); elnavegante, 4–5; Ilya Shulika, 21 (alien); M. Cornelius, 26 (background); NikolayN, 28–29; Thomas Bethge, 32; SuperStock: Transtock / Transtock, 6
Every effort has been made to contact copyright holders for material reproduced in this book. Any omissions will be rectified in subsequent printings if notice is given to the publisher.

Contents

CHAPTER 1
What Is Area 51?......4

CHAPTER 2
History of Area 51......8

CHAPTER 3
Aliens at Area 51......16

CHAPTER 4
Area 51 Skeptics......23

Other Resources...........30

What Is Area 51?

In 2014, a strange video appeared online. In it, an old man spoke to the camera. His name was Boyd Bushman. He held up photos as he spoke. He said they were of spaceships. He held up more photos. These were of a weird creature. He said it was an alien. Bushman said the photos were taken at a place called Area 51.

JUL · 73Y

Signs around Area 51 warn people to stay out. They say, "Use of deadly force authorized."

6

Top Secret

Bushman, a **retired engineer**, believed aliens were real. He said they could be found at Area 51.

Area 51 is a secret U.S. government space. It is in the Nevada desert. No cameras are allowed there. None of the buildings have windows. Planes can't fly overhead. Guards **patrol** the area.

Area 51 is off-limits to almost everyone. People need military **clearance** to enter. For a long time, Area 51 couldn't be found on any maps.

CHAPTER 2

History of

Area 51 was built in 1955. People wondered why it was so secret. No one knew what the government was doing or why. The government didn't even admit that Area 51 was real until 2013.

Area 51 is by Groom Lake. There is no water in the lake. It dried up thousands of years ago. Now, it is used as a runway for airplanes.

MAP OF AREA 51

RACHEL
(closest town)

GROOM LAKE

TIKABOO PEAK
26 miles (42 kilometers) away
It is the closest people can get
to Area 51.

DORMITORIES

BASEBALL FIELD

NEW RUNWAY

OLD RUNWAY

NEVADA NATIONAL SECURITY TEST SITE

PLANE HANGARS

Secret Projects

The government says it builds weapons and aircraft at Area 51. In the 1950s and 1960s, people there made planes to spy on other countries. The government did not want other countries to know about the planes. It kept Area 51 a secret.

Some people have seen strange things flying over Area 51. Are they really airplanes? Or are they something else?

SR-71
BLACKBIRD

TOP SPEED
2,200 MILES
(3,541 KM) PER HOUR

**TOP SPEED
646 MILES
(1,040 KM) PER HOUR**

F-117A
NIGHTHAWK
STEALTH PLANE

U-2
SPY PLANE

**TOP SPEED
410 MILES
(660 KM) PER HOUR**

CHAPTER 3

Aliens at

In 1947, something strange crashed near Roswell, New Mexico. The U.S. government said it was a weather balloon. But some people believe it was a spaceship. They think the government took it to Area 51.

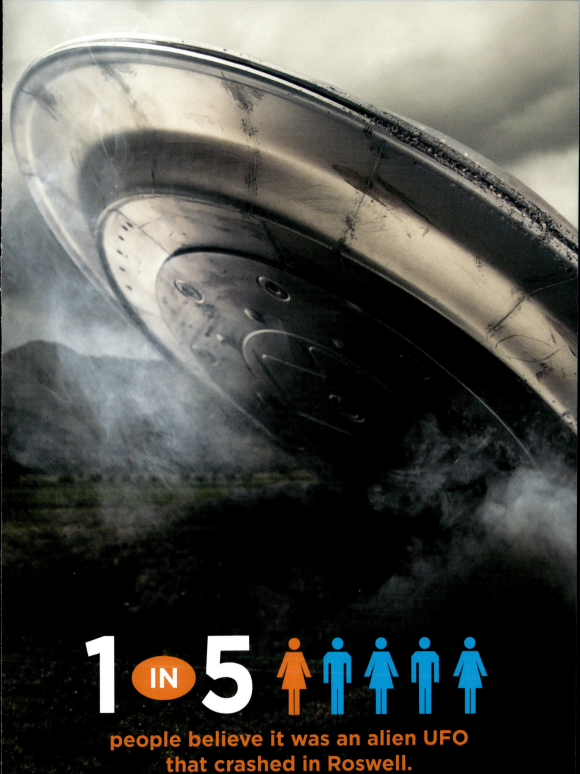

1 IN 5

people believe it was an alien UFO
that crashed in Roswell.

Robert Lazar

In 1989, Robert Lazar went on TV. He said he worked on alien technology at Area 51. Lazar said Area 51 had nine spaceships. Before his interview, few people knew about Area 51.

Some people believe Lazar. They say his story never changed. Others don't believe him. There are no records of where he worked or went to school. Did he lie about it all? Or did the government erase the records?

Believers

Some people think scientists study spaceships at Area 51. They say the government uses alien technology. They think it's used to build weapons and aircraft. Some believe Bushman's pictures are real.

The secret projects at Area 51 are called black projects.

BOYD BUSHMAN'S ALIEN

NO HAIR

LARGE BLACK EYES

LONG FINGERS

WEBBED TOES

ABOUT 4.5 TO 5 FEET (137 TO 152 CENTIMETERS) TALL

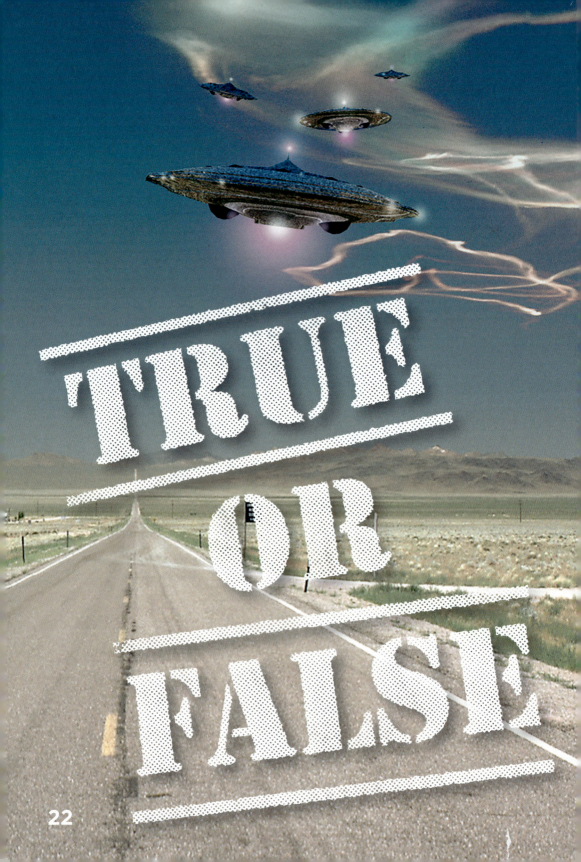

TRUE OR FALSE

CHAPTER 4

Area 51 Skeptics

Skeptics don't think Area 51 has anything to do with aliens. They say Lazar lied. They say Bushman's pictures are fake. His alien looks a lot like a toy sold in stores.

Just Airplanes

Many people say Area 51 is top secret for a good reason. The military is building and testing new airplanes. Sometimes people see them flying. They mistake the planes for spaceships.

HOW MANY PEOPLE BELIEVE IN UFOS?

36% OF AMERICANS BELIEVE IN UFOS

17% DO NOT

47% AREN'T SURE

You Decide

Some people believe the case for aliens at Area 51 isn't very good. They ask why aliens in pictures look like toys. They ask why there isn't any proof.

Those who believe think the photos are real. They believe the **witnesses'** stories. They wonder why Area 51 is secret if it only has airplanes.

Will people ever learn the truth?

Believe It or Not?

Answer the questions below. Then add up your points to see if you believe.

1 You see something strange flying over Area 51. What do you think?

A. It must be an alien spaceship! **(3 points)**

B. I wonder what it is. **(2 points)**

C. What a cool airplane! **(1 point)**

2 Read page 19 again. What do you think about Lazar?

A. He must be telling the truth. **(3 points)**

B. I'd like to know more. **(2 points)**

C. He probably made it all up. **(1 point)**

3 Do you believe in aliens?

A. Of course I do. **(3 points)**

B. I haven't decided yet. **(2 points)**

C. Don't be silly! **(1 point)**

3 points
There's no way Area 51 has aliens.

4–8 points
Maybe it does. But then again, maybe it doesn't.

9 points
You're a total believer!

GLOSSARY

authorize (AW-thuh-rahyz)—to give power or permission to do something

clearance (KLEER-uhns)—permission to access secret information, such as documents or photos

dormitory (DAWR-mi-tor-ee)—a large room with many beds where people can sleep

engineer (ehn-juh-NEER)—a person who designs and creates things using scientific methods

patrol (puh-TROHL)—going around an area to make sure it is safe

retired (ree-TIY-rd)—not working anymore

skeptic (SKEP-tik)—a person who questions something

stealth (STELTH)—an aircraft design that is hard for radar to pick up

witness (WIT-nes)—someone who sees something happen

BOOKS

Karst, Ken. *Area 51*. Enduring Mysteries. Mankato, MN: Creative Education, 2015.

Krasner, Barbara. *The Mystery of Area 51*. Mysteries of History. Minneapolis: Core Library, an imprint of Abdo Publishing, 2016.

Linde, Barbara M. *What Happened at Area 51?* History's Mysteries. New York: Gareth Stevens Publishing, 2015.

WEBSITES

Amy's Aviation: SR-71 Blackbird
www.funkidslive.com/learn/amys-aviation/amys-aviation-sr-71-blackbird/

Do Aliens Really Exist?
discoverykids.com/articles/do-aliens-really-exist/

UFO Facts
kidskonnect.com/science/ufo/

INDEX

A

aircraft, 9, 10–11, 13, 14–15, 20, 24, 27

aliens, 4, 7, 19, 20–21, 23, 27

B

Bushman, Boyd, 4, 7, 20–21, 23

H

history, 8, 13, 16

L

Lazar, Robert, 19, 23

location, 7, 9, 10–11

S

security, 6, 7

skeptics, 23, 24, 25, 27

spaceships, 4, 16, 17, 19, 20, 24, 25

U

U.S. government, 7, 8, 13, 16, 19, 20, 24